50 Low-Carb Pasta Alternatives

By: Kelly Johnson

Table of Contents

- Zucchini Noodles with Pesto
- Spaghetti Squash Marinara
- Cauliflower Mac and Cheese
- Shirataki Noodle Stir-Fry
- Eggplant Lasagna
- Cabbage Noodle Beef Stroganoff
- Almond Flour Pasta
- Spaghetti Squash Pad Thai
- Butternut Squash Noodles
- Broccoli Rabe and Sausage Pasta
- Zoodle Alfredo
- Cabbage Roll Casserole
- Carrot Noodles with Ginger Sauce
- Spaghetti Squash Carbonara
- Radish Pasta with Garlic Butter
- Creamy Cauliflower Pasta
- Zucchini and Bell Pepper Frittata
- Eggplant Fettuccine
- Portobello Mushroom Lasagna
- Spinach and Ricotta Stuffed Zucchini
- Konjac Noodles with Bolognese Sauce
- Chicken Alfredo with Zucchini Noodles
- Avocado and Basil Zoodles
- Cauliflower Gnocchi
- Roasted Vegetable Spiral Pasta
- Cabbage and Sausage Skillet
- Zucchini and Shrimp Scampi
- Eggplant and Tomato Bake
- Asian Zoodle Salad
- Stuffed Bell Peppers with Cauliflower Rice
- Pesto Zoodles with Cherry Tomatoes
- Coconut Flour Noodles
- Spicy Cabbage and Sausage Pasta
- Mushroom and Spinach Zoodle Bake
- Zucchini Lasagna Roll-Ups

- Beet Noodles with Goat Cheese
- Almond Flour Gnocchi
- Cabbage Noodles with Peanut Sauce
- Cauliflower Fried Rice with Shrimp
- Zucchini Fettuccine with Marinara Sauce
- Spinach and Feta Stuffed Eggplant
- Spaghetti Squash with Meatballs
- Egg Noodles with Alfredo Sauce
- Cheesy Broccoli and Cauliflower Bake
- Zoodle Taco Salad
- Radish Pasta with Lemon Garlic Sauce
- Spinach and Mushroom Stuffed Peppers
- Zucchini and Bacon Frittata
- Eggplant Rollatini
- Pesto Shirataki Noodles

Zucchini Noodles with Pesto

Ingredients:

- 4 medium zucchinis
- 1 cup basil pesto (store-bought or homemade)
- 1/2 cup cherry tomatoes, halved
- 1/4 cup grated Parmesan cheese
- Salt and pepper to taste
- Olive oil for drizzling

Instructions:

1. **Prepare the zucchini**: Use a spiralizer or vegetable peeler to create zucchini noodles.
2. **Cook the noodles**: In a skillet, heat a drizzle of olive oil over medium heat. Add the zucchini noodles and sauté for 2-3 minutes until just tender.
3. **Mix with pesto**: Remove from heat, and toss the zucchini noodles with pesto, cherry tomatoes, salt, and pepper.
4. **Serve**: Plate the noodles, sprinkle with Parmesan cheese, and drizzle with olive oil before serving.

Spaghetti Squash Marinara

Ingredients:

- 1 medium spaghetti squash
- 2 cups marinara sauce (store-bought or homemade)
- 1/2 cup grated Parmesan cheese
- Fresh basil for garnish
- Salt and pepper to taste

Instructions:

1. **Cook the squash**: Preheat the oven to 400°F (200°C). Cut the spaghetti squash in half lengthwise and remove seeds. Place cut side down on a baking sheet and roast for 40-45 minutes until tender.
2. **Prepare marinara**: In a saucepan, heat marinara sauce over medium heat.
3. **Scrape squash**: Once cooked, use a fork to scrape the inside of the squash, creating spaghetti-like strands.
4. **Combine**: In a bowl, mix the spaghetti squash strands with marinara sauce, salt, and pepper.
5. **Serve**: Plate and sprinkle with Parmesan cheese and fresh basil before serving.

Cauliflower Mac and Cheese

Ingredients:

- 1 medium head cauliflower, cut into florets
- 1 cup shredded cheddar cheese
- 1/2 cup cream cheese
- 1/2 cup milk
- 1/2 tsp garlic powder
- Salt and pepper to taste
- 1/2 cup breadcrumbs (optional)

Instructions:

1. **Cook cauliflower**: Steam or boil cauliflower florets until tender, about 5-7 minutes. Drain and set aside.
2. **Make cheese sauce**: In a saucepan, combine shredded cheddar, cream cheese, milk, garlic powder, salt, and pepper over medium heat until melted and smooth.
3. **Combine**: Mix cooked cauliflower with the cheese sauce until well coated.
4. **Bake (optional)**: If desired, transfer to a baking dish, top with breadcrumbs, and bake at 350°F (175°C) for 15-20 minutes until golden and bubbly.

Shirataki Noodle Stir-Fry

Ingredients:

- 1 package (7 oz) shirataki noodles, rinsed and drained
- 1 cup mixed vegetables (bell peppers, carrots, broccoli)
- 2 cloves garlic, minced
- 2 tbsp soy sauce
- 1 tbsp sesame oil
- 1/2 tsp crushed red pepper flakes (optional)

Instructions:

1. **Prepare noodles**: In a skillet, heat sesame oil over medium-high heat. Add minced garlic and stir-fry for 30 seconds.
2. **Add vegetables**: Add mixed vegetables and stir-fry for 3-4 minutes until tender.
3. **Add noodles**: Stir in shirataki noodles and soy sauce, cooking for another 2-3 minutes until heated through.
4. **Serve**: Sprinkle with crushed red pepper flakes if desired and serve hot.

Eggplant Lasagna

Ingredients:

- 2 medium eggplants, sliced into thin rounds
- 2 cups marinara sauce
- 1 cup ricotta cheese
- 1 1/2 cups shredded mozzarella cheese
- 1/2 cup grated Parmesan cheese
- 1 egg
- Salt and pepper to taste
- Olive oil for brushing

Instructions:

1. **Prepare eggplant**: Preheat the oven to 375°F (190°C). Brush eggplant slices with olive oil and season with salt. Arrange on a baking sheet and roast for 20 minutes.
2. **Make cheese mixture**: In a bowl, combine ricotta cheese, egg, salt, and pepper.
3. **Layer lasagna**: In a baking dish, spread a layer of marinara sauce, followed by a layer of roasted eggplant, ricotta mixture, and mozzarella. Repeat layers, finishing with marinara and mozzarella on top.
4. **Bake**: Bake for 30-35 minutes until bubbly and golden. Let cool for a few minutes before serving.

Cabbage Noodle Beef Stroganoff

Ingredients:

- 1 small head of cabbage, shredded
- 1 lb (450g) ground beef
- 1 onion, diced
- 2 cloves garlic, minced
- 1 cup beef broth
- 1 cup sour cream
- 1 tbsp Worcestershire sauce
- Salt and pepper to taste

Instructions:

1. **Cook beef**: In a large skillet, brown ground beef over medium heat. Drain excess fat.
2. **Add vegetables**: Add onion and garlic, cooking until soft.
3. **Combine ingredients**: Stir in beef broth, Worcestershire sauce, salt, and pepper. Bring to a simmer.
4. **Add cabbage**: Stir in shredded cabbage, cooking until tender, about 5-7 minutes.
5. **Finish**: Remove from heat and stir in sour cream until well combined. Serve hot.

Almond Flour Pasta

Ingredients:

- 2 cups almond flour
- 2 large eggs
- 1/4 tsp salt
- 1 tbsp olive oil
- Water as needed

Instructions:

1. **Make dough**: In a bowl, combine almond flour, eggs, salt, and olive oil. Mix until a dough forms. If too crumbly, add a little water until it holds together.
2. **Roll out**: On a floured surface, roll out the dough to your desired thickness.
3. **Cut pasta**: Cut into desired shapes (fettuccine, lasagna sheets, etc.).
4. **Cook pasta**: Boil in salted water for 2-3 minutes until cooked through. Drain and serve with your favorite sauce.

Spaghetti Squash Pad Thai

Ingredients:

- 1 medium spaghetti squash
- 2 eggs, beaten
- 1 cup bean sprouts
- 1/2 cup green onions, chopped
- 1/4 cup peanuts, chopped
- 3 tbsp soy sauce
- 2 tbsp peanut butter
- 1 tbsp lime juice
- 1 tsp sriracha (optional)
- Olive oil for cooking

Instructions:

1. **Cook squash**: Preheat the oven to 400°F (200°C). Cut spaghetti squash in half, remove seeds, and roast cut side down for 40-45 minutes until tender.
2. **Prepare sauce**: In a bowl, mix soy sauce, peanut butter, lime juice, and sriracha if using.
3. **Scramble eggs**: In a skillet, heat olive oil over medium heat. Scramble the beaten eggs and set aside.
4. **Combine ingredients**: Once the squash is cooked, scrape out the strands and add to the skillet. Stir in bean sprouts, green onions, scrambled eggs, and sauce.
5. **Serve**: Top with chopped peanuts before serving.

Feel free to ask for more recipes or any adjustments!

Butternut Squash Noodles

Ingredients:

- 1 medium butternut squash
- 2 tbsp olive oil
- Salt and pepper to taste
- 1/2 cup grated Parmesan cheese
- Fresh herbs for garnish (optional)

Instructions:

1. **Prepare squash**: Preheat the oven to 400°F (200°C). Cut the butternut squash in half lengthwise, remove seeds, and drizzle with olive oil, salt, and pepper.
2. **Roast**: Place cut side down on a baking sheet and roast for 30-40 minutes until tender.
3. **Make noodles**: Once cooked, scoop out the flesh and spiralize it into noodles.
4. **Serve**: Toss with Parmesan cheese and fresh herbs before serving.

Broccoli Rabe and Sausage Pasta

Ingredients:

- 8 oz pasta (your choice)
- 1 lb Italian sausage, casings removed
- 1 bunch broccoli rabe, trimmed and chopped
- 2 cloves garlic, minced
- 1/2 tsp red pepper flakes (optional)
- Olive oil
- Salt and pepper to taste
- Grated Parmesan cheese for serving

Instructions:

1. **Cook pasta**: Cook pasta according to package instructions until al dente. Reserve 1/2 cup pasta water and drain.
2. **Cook sausage**: In a skillet, heat olive oil over medium heat. Add sausage and cook until browned.
3. **Add garlic and broccoli**: Stir in garlic and broccoli rabe, cooking until the broccoli is tender, about 5 minutes.
4. **Combine**: Add cooked pasta to the skillet along with reserved pasta water, red pepper flakes, salt, and pepper. Toss to combine.
5. **Serve**: Plate and sprinkle with grated Parmesan cheese before serving.

Zoodle Alfredo

Ingredients:

- 4 medium zucchinis
- 1 cup heavy cream
- 1 cup grated Parmesan cheese
- 2 cloves garlic, minced
- Salt and pepper to taste
- Olive oil for cooking
- Fresh parsley for garnish

Instructions:

1. **Prepare zucchinis**: Use a spiralizer to create zucchini noodles (zoodles).
2. **Cook zoodles**: In a skillet, heat olive oil over medium heat. Add zoodles and sauté for 2-3 minutes until just tender. Remove and set aside.
3. **Make Alfredo sauce**: In the same skillet, add garlic and cook for 30 seconds. Pour in heavy cream, bringing it to a simmer. Stir in Parmesan cheese, salt, and pepper until smooth.
4. **Combine**: Add zoodles back to the skillet and toss to coat with the Alfredo sauce.
5. **Serve**: Garnish with fresh parsley before serving.

Cabbage Roll Casserole

Ingredients:

- 1 medium head cabbage, chopped
- 1 lb ground beef or turkey
- 1 onion, diced
- 2 cups marinara sauce
- 1 cup cooked rice
- 1 tsp garlic powder
- Salt and pepper to taste
- 1/2 cup shredded cheese (optional)

Instructions:

1. **Preheat oven**: Preheat the oven to 350°F (175°C).
2. **Cook meat**: In a skillet, brown ground beef or turkey with onion until cooked through. Drain excess fat.
3. **Mix ingredients**: In a large bowl, combine cooked meat, cabbage, marinara sauce, rice, garlic powder, salt, and pepper.
4. **Transfer to baking dish**: Pour mixture into a greased casserole dish and cover with foil.
5. **Bake**: Bake for 45 minutes. If using cheese, uncover and sprinkle on top for the last 10 minutes until melted and bubbly.

Carrot Noodles with Ginger Sauce

Ingredients:

- 4 medium carrots
- 2 tbsp soy sauce
- 1 tbsp ginger, grated
- 1 tbsp sesame oil
- 1 tsp honey or maple syrup
- Salt and pepper to taste
- Sesame seeds for garnish

Instructions:

1. **Make carrot noodles**: Use a spiralizer to create carrot noodles.
2. **Prepare sauce**: In a bowl, mix soy sauce, ginger, sesame oil, honey, salt, and pepper.
3. **Cook noodles**: In a skillet, add carrot noodles and sauté for 3-4 minutes until tender.
4. **Combine**: Remove from heat and toss with ginger sauce.
5. **Serve**: Garnish with sesame seeds before serving.

Spaghetti Squash Carbonara

Ingredients:

- 1 medium spaghetti squash
- 4 slices bacon, diced
- 2 large eggs
- 1/2 cup grated Parmesan cheese
- 1/2 tsp black pepper
- Fresh parsley for garnish

Instructions:

1. **Cook squash**: Preheat the oven to 400°F (200°C). Cut the spaghetti squash in half, remove seeds, and roast cut side down for 30-40 minutes until tender.
2. **Cook bacon**: In a skillet, cook bacon over medium heat until crispy. Remove and drain on paper towels.
3. **Scrape squash**: Once cooked, scrape the inside of the squash to create spaghetti-like strands.
4. **Make sauce**: In a bowl, whisk together eggs, Parmesan cheese, and black pepper.
5. **Combine**: In the skillet with bacon drippings, add spaghetti squash, remove from heat, and quickly stir in the egg mixture until creamy. Top with bacon and garnish with parsley.

Radish Pasta with Garlic Butter

Ingredients:

- 1 bunch radishes, sliced thinly
- 2 tbsp butter
- 2 cloves garlic, minced
- Salt and pepper to taste
- Fresh herbs for garnish (optional)

Instructions:

1. **Cook radishes**: In a skillet, melt butter over medium heat. Add sliced radishes and sauté for about 5 minutes until tender.
2. **Add garlic**: Stir in garlic and cook for another 1-2 minutes until fragrant.
3. **Season**: Season with salt and pepper.
4. **Serve**: Garnish with fresh herbs if desired before serving.

Creamy Cauliflower Pasta

Ingredients:

- 1 medium head cauliflower, chopped
- 8 oz pasta of choice
- 1 cup vegetable broth
- 1/2 cup cream or Greek yogurt
- 2 cloves garlic, minced
- Salt and pepper to taste
- Grated Parmesan cheese for serving

Instructions:

1. **Cook pasta**: Cook pasta according to package instructions.
2. **Steam cauliflower**: Steam cauliflower until tender, about 5-7 minutes.
3. **Make sauce**: In a blender, combine steamed cauliflower, vegetable broth, cream or yogurt, garlic, salt, and pepper. Blend until smooth.
4. **Combine**: In a pot, mix cooked pasta with the creamy cauliflower sauce, heating through.
5. **Serve**: Plate and sprinkle with grated Parmesan cheese before serving.

Feel free to let me know if you need any more recipes or adjustments!

Zucchini and Bell Pepper Frittata

Ingredients:

- 6 large eggs
- 1 medium zucchini, diced
- 1 bell pepper, diced (any color)
- 1/2 onion, diced
- 1/2 cup shredded cheese (optional)
- Salt and pepper to taste
- 2 tbsp olive oil
- Fresh herbs for garnish (optional)

Instructions:

1. **Preheat oven**: Preheat the oven to 350°F (175°C).
2. **Cook vegetables**: In an oven-safe skillet, heat olive oil over medium heat. Add onion, zucchini, and bell pepper, cooking until softened, about 5-7 minutes.
3. **Prepare eggs**: In a bowl, whisk together eggs, salt, and pepper. Pour the egg mixture over the cooked vegetables in the skillet.
4. **Cook frittata**: If using cheese, sprinkle on top. Cook on the stove for 2-3 minutes until the edges set, then transfer to the oven and bake for 15-20 minutes until fully set.
5. **Serve**: Let cool slightly before slicing. Garnish with fresh herbs if desired.

Eggplant Fettuccine

Ingredients:

- 2 medium eggplants
- 1 cup marinara sauce
- 1/2 cup grated Parmesan cheese
- 2 cloves garlic, minced
- Olive oil for cooking
- Salt and pepper to taste
- Fresh basil for garnish (optional)

Instructions:

1. **Prepare eggplant**: Cut eggplants into long strips to resemble fettuccine noodles.
2. **Cook noodles**: In a skillet, heat olive oil over medium heat. Add eggplant strips and sauté until tender, about 5-7 minutes.
3. **Add sauce**: Stir in marinara sauce and garlic, cooking for another 2-3 minutes. Season with salt and pepper.
4. **Serve**: Plate the eggplant fettuccine and top with grated Parmesan cheese and fresh basil if desired.

Portobello Mushroom Lasagna

Ingredients:

- 8 large portobello mushrooms, stems removed
- 2 cups ricotta cheese
- 2 cups marinara sauce
- 2 cups shredded mozzarella cheese
- 1/2 cup grated Parmesan cheese
- 1 egg
- 1 tsp Italian seasoning
- Salt and pepper to taste

Instructions:

1. **Preheat oven**: Preheat the oven to 375°F (190°C).
2. **Prepare filling**: In a bowl, mix ricotta cheese, egg, Italian seasoning, salt, and pepper.
3. **Layer ingredients**: In a baking dish, spread a layer of marinara sauce, then layer portobello mushrooms, ricotta mixture, and mozzarella cheese. Repeat layers until all ingredients are used, finishing with marinara sauce and mozzarella on top.
4. **Bake**: Cover with foil and bake for 25 minutes. Remove foil and bake for an additional 10-15 minutes until bubbly and golden.
5. **Serve**: Let cool slightly before slicing and serving.

Spinach and Ricotta Stuffed Zucchini

Ingredients:

- 4 medium zucchinis
- 1 cup ricotta cheese
- 2 cups fresh spinach, chopped
- 1/2 cup grated Parmesan cheese
- 1 tsp garlic powder
- Salt and pepper to taste
- Marinara sauce for serving

Instructions:

1. **Preheat oven**: Preheat the oven to 375°F (190°C).
2. **Prepare zucchinis**: Cut zucchinis in half lengthwise and scoop out the insides to create boats.
3. **Make filling**: In a bowl, mix ricotta cheese, chopped spinach, Parmesan cheese, garlic powder, salt, and pepper.
4. **Stuff zucchinis**: Fill each zucchini half with the ricotta mixture and place in a baking dish.
5. **Bake**: Bake for 20-25 minutes until zucchinis are tender. Serve with marinara sauce.

Konjac Noodles with Bolognese Sauce

Ingredients:

- 1 package konjac noodles, drained and rinsed
- 1 lb ground beef or turkey
- 1 cup marinara sauce
- 1 onion, diced
- 2 cloves garlic, minced
- Olive oil for cooking
- Salt and pepper to taste
- Fresh basil for garnish (optional)

Instructions:

1. **Cook meat**: In a skillet, heat olive oil over medium heat. Add onion and garlic, cooking until fragrant. Add ground meat and cook until browned.
2. **Add sauce**: Stir in marinara sauce and let simmer for 10 minutes. Season with salt and pepper.
3. **Prepare noodles**: In a separate pot, heat konjac noodles according to package instructions.
4. **Combine**: Serve Bolognese sauce over konjac noodles and garnish with fresh basil if desired.

Chicken Alfredo with Zucchini Noodles

Ingredients:

- 2 medium zucchinis, spiralized
- 1 lb cooked chicken breast, shredded
- 1 cup heavy cream
- 1/2 cup grated Parmesan cheese
- 2 cloves garlic, minced
- Salt and pepper to taste
- Olive oil for cooking

Instructions:

1. **Cook zoodles**: In a skillet, heat olive oil over medium heat. Add zucchini noodles and sauté for 2-3 minutes until tender. Remove and set aside.
2. **Make Alfredo sauce**: In the same skillet, add garlic and cook for 30 seconds. Pour in heavy cream, bringing it to a simmer. Stir in Parmesan cheese, salt, and pepper until smooth.
3. **Combine**: Add cooked chicken and zoodles back into the skillet, tossing to coat in the Alfredo sauce.
4. **Serve**: Plate and serve immediately.

Avocado and Basil Zoodles

Ingredients:

- 4 medium zucchinis
- 1 ripe avocado
- 2 cloves garlic
- Juice of 1 lemon
- 1/4 cup fresh basil leaves
- Salt and pepper to taste

Instructions:

1. **Make zoodles**: Spiralize the zucchinis into noodles.
2. **Make sauce**: In a blender, combine avocado, garlic, lemon juice, basil, salt, and pepper. Blend until smooth.
3. **Toss noodles**: In a bowl, toss zoodles with the avocado sauce until evenly coated.
4. **Serve**: Serve fresh, garnished with extra basil if desired.

Cauliflower Gnocchi

Ingredients:

- 1 medium head cauliflower, steamed and mashed
- 1 cup almond flour
- 1/2 cup grated Parmesan cheese
- 1 egg
- Salt to taste
- Olive oil for cooking

Instructions:

1. **Prepare dough**: In a bowl, mix mashed cauliflower, almond flour, Parmesan cheese, egg, and salt until a dough forms.
2. **Shape gnocchi**: Divide the dough into small pieces and roll into logs. Cut into small gnocchi pieces.
3. **Cook gnocchi**: In a skillet, heat olive oil over medium heat. Add gnocchi and cook until golden brown, about 3-4 minutes per side.
4. **Serve**: Serve with your favorite sauce or seasoning.

Feel free to ask if you need any additional recipes or modifications!

Roasted Vegetable Spiral Pasta

Ingredients:

- 8 oz spiral pasta (gluten-free if desired)
- 2 cups mixed vegetables (bell peppers, zucchini, carrots)
- 2 tbsp olive oil
- 1 tsp Italian seasoning
- Salt and pepper to taste
- Grated Parmesan cheese for serving (optional)

Instructions:

1. **Preheat oven**: Preheat the oven to 400°F (200°C).
2. **Roast vegetables**: Toss mixed vegetables with olive oil, Italian seasoning, salt, and pepper. Spread on a baking sheet and roast for 20-25 minutes until tender.
3. **Cook pasta**: Cook pasta according to package instructions. Drain and set aside.
4. **Combine**: In a large bowl, mix roasted vegetables with pasta. Serve with grated Parmesan cheese if desired.

Cabbage and Sausage Skillet

Ingredients:

- 1 lb smoked sausage, sliced
- 4 cups cabbage, chopped
- 1 onion, diced
- 2 cloves garlic, minced
- 2 tbsp olive oil
- Salt and pepper to taste

Instructions:

1. **Cook sausage**: In a large skillet, heat olive oil over medium heat. Add sliced sausage and cook until browned, about 5-7 minutes.
2. **Add vegetables**: Add onion and garlic, cooking until fragrant. Stir in cabbage and cook until wilted, about 10 minutes.
3. **Season**: Season with salt and pepper. Serve hot.

Zucchini and Shrimp Scampi

Ingredients:

- 2 medium zucchinis, spiralized
- 1 lb shrimp, peeled and deveined
- 4 cloves garlic, minced
- 1/4 cup chicken broth
- Juice of 1 lemon
- 2 tbsp olive oil
- Salt and pepper to taste
- Fresh parsley for garnish (optional)

Instructions:

1. **Cook shrimp**: In a skillet, heat olive oil over medium heat. Add garlic and cook for 30 seconds, then add shrimp. Cook until pink, about 3-4 minutes.
2. **Add broth and zucchini**: Pour in chicken broth and lemon juice. Add zucchini noodles and toss for 2-3 minutes until heated through.
3. **Serve**: Season with salt and pepper. Garnish with fresh parsley if desired.

Eggplant and Tomato Bake

Ingredients:

- 2 medium eggplants, sliced
- 4 tomatoes, sliced
- 1 cup mozzarella cheese, shredded
- 1/2 cup Parmesan cheese, grated
- 2 cloves garlic, minced
- 2 tbsp olive oil
- Salt and pepper to taste
- Fresh basil for garnish (optional)

Instructions:

1. **Preheat oven**: Preheat the oven to 375°F (190°C).
2. **Layer ingredients**: In a baking dish, layer eggplant and tomato slices, sprinkling garlic, salt, and pepper between layers. Top with mozzarella and Parmesan cheese.
3. **Bake**: Bake for 30-35 minutes until golden and bubbly.
4. **Serve**: Garnish with fresh basil if desired.

Asian Zoodle Salad

Ingredients:

- 4 medium zucchinis, spiralized
- 1 cup carrots, julienned
- 1 bell pepper, sliced
- 1/4 cup soy sauce (or tamari for gluten-free)
- 2 tbsp sesame oil
- 1 tbsp rice vinegar
- Sesame seeds for garnish

Instructions:

1. **Prepare vegetables**: In a large bowl, combine zucchini noodles, carrots, and bell pepper.
2. **Make dressing**: In a separate bowl, whisk together soy sauce, sesame oil, and rice vinegar.
3. **Toss salad**: Pour dressing over the vegetables and toss to coat.
4. **Serve**: Garnish with sesame seeds before serving.

Stuffed Bell Peppers with Cauliflower Rice

Ingredients:

- 4 bell peppers, halved and seeds removed
- 2 cups cauliflower rice
- 1 lb ground turkey or beef
- 1 cup marinara sauce
- 1 tsp Italian seasoning
- Salt and pepper to taste
- Grated cheese for topping (optional)

Instructions:

1. **Preheat oven**: Preheat the oven to 375°F (190°C).
2. **Cook filling**: In a skillet, cook ground turkey or beef until browned. Stir in cauliflower rice, marinara sauce, Italian seasoning, salt, and pepper.
3. **Stuff peppers**: Fill each bell pepper half with the meat mixture. Place in a baking dish and top with cheese if desired.
4. **Bake**: Bake for 25-30 minutes until the peppers are tender.

Pesto Zoodles with Cherry Tomatoes

Ingredients:

- 4 medium zucchinis, spiralized
- 1 cup cherry tomatoes, halved
- 1/2 cup pesto sauce (store-bought or homemade)
- 2 tbsp olive oil
- Salt and pepper to taste
- Grated Parmesan cheese for serving (optional)

Instructions:

1. **Sauté zoodles**: In a skillet, heat olive oil over medium heat. Add zucchini noodles and sauté for 2-3 minutes until just tender.
2. **Add tomatoes**: Stir in cherry tomatoes and cook for an additional 2 minutes.
3. **Mix with pesto**: Remove from heat and toss with pesto sauce. Season with salt and pepper.
4. **Serve**: Serve with grated Parmesan cheese if desired.

Coconut Flour Noodles

Ingredients:

- 1 cup coconut flour
- 1/4 cup water
- 2 large eggs
- 1/2 tsp salt

Instructions:

1. **Make dough**: In a bowl, mix coconut flour, water, eggs, and salt until a dough forms.
2. **Roll out**: On a floured surface, roll out the dough to your desired thickness.
3. **Cut noodles**: Cut into desired noodle shapes.
4. **Cook noodles**: Boil in salted water for 3-4 minutes until cooked through. Drain and serve with sauce of choice.

Feel free to ask if you need more recipes or further assistance!

Spicy Cabbage and Sausage Pasta

Ingredients:

- 8 oz pasta (gluten-free if desired)
- 1 lb smoked sausage, sliced
- 4 cups cabbage, chopped
- 1 onion, diced
- 2 cloves garlic, minced
- 1/2 tsp red pepper flakes
- 2 tbsp olive oil
- Salt and pepper to taste
- Fresh parsley for garnish (optional)

Instructions:

1. **Cook pasta**: Boil pasta according to package instructions. Drain and set aside.
2. **Cook sausage**: In a large skillet, heat olive oil over medium heat. Add sliced sausage and cook until browned, about 5-7 minutes.
3. **Add vegetables**: Add onion, garlic, and red pepper flakes. Cook until onions are soft.
4. **Combine**: Stir in chopped cabbage and cooked pasta. Season with salt and pepper. Cook until cabbage is wilted.
5. **Serve**: Garnish with fresh parsley if desired.

Mushroom and Spinach Zoodle Bake

Ingredients:

- 4 medium zucchinis, spiralized
- 2 cups mushrooms, sliced
- 2 cups spinach, chopped
- 1 cup ricotta cheese
- 1 cup mozzarella cheese, shredded
- 1/2 cup Parmesan cheese, grated
- 2 cloves garlic, minced
- Salt and pepper to taste

Instructions:

1. **Preheat oven**: Preheat the oven to 375°F (190°C).
2. **Sauté vegetables**: In a skillet, heat olive oil over medium heat. Add mushrooms and garlic, cooking until mushrooms are tender. Stir in spinach and cook until wilted.
3. **Combine**: In a baking dish, layer zoodles, ricotta, sautéed vegetables, and mozzarella. Repeat layers, finishing with mozzarella and Parmesan on top.
4. **Bake**: Bake for 25-30 minutes until golden and bubbly.

Zucchini Lasagna Roll-Ups

Ingredients:

- 4 medium zucchinis, thinly sliced
- 2 cups marinara sauce
- 1 cup ricotta cheese
- 1 cup mozzarella cheese, shredded
- 1/2 cup Parmesan cheese, grated
- 1 egg
- 1 tsp Italian seasoning
- Salt and pepper to taste

Instructions:

1. **Preheat oven**: Preheat the oven to 375°F (190°C).
2. **Prepare filling**: In a bowl, mix ricotta cheese, egg, Italian seasoning, salt, and pepper.
3. **Roll up**: Spread marinara sauce on a baking dish. Place zucchini slices on a flat surface, add a spoonful of filling, and roll up. Place seam-side down in the dish.
4. **Top and bake**: Cover with remaining marinara sauce and sprinkle with mozzarella and Parmesan. Bake for 25-30 minutes until heated through.

Beet Noodles with Goat Cheese

Ingredients:

- 4 medium beets, spiralized
- 2 tbsp olive oil
- 1/4 cup goat cheese, crumbled
- 1/4 cup walnuts, chopped
- 2 tbsp balsamic vinegar
- Salt and pepper to taste

Instructions:

1. **Sauté beets**: In a skillet, heat olive oil over medium heat. Add spiralized beets and sauté for 5-7 minutes until tender.
2. **Mix dressing**: In a bowl, whisk together balsamic vinegar, salt, and pepper.
3. **Combine**: Toss beets with dressing, walnuts, and goat cheese. Serve warm or at room temperature.

Almond Flour Gnocchi

Ingredients:

- 2 cups almond flour
- 1 cup ricotta cheese
- 1 egg
- 1/2 tsp salt
- 1/4 tsp nutmeg

Instructions:

1. **Make dough**: In a bowl, combine almond flour, ricotta, egg, salt, and nutmeg. Mix until a dough forms.
2. **Shape gnocchi**: Divide dough into small pieces and roll into logs. Cut into bite-sized pieces.
3. **Cook gnocchi**: Boil a pot of salted water. Cook gnocchi until they float to the surface, about 2-3 minutes. Drain.
4. **Serve**: Toss with sauce of choice.

Cabbage Noodles with Peanut Sauce

Ingredients:

- 4 cups cabbage, shredded
- 1/4 cup peanut butter
- 2 tbsp soy sauce (or tamari for gluten-free)
- 1 tbsp honey or maple syrup
- 1 clove garlic, minced
- 1 tbsp lime juice
- 2 tbsp water
- Chopped peanuts and green onions for garnish

Instructions:

1. **Sauté cabbage**: In a skillet, sauté cabbage in a little oil over medium heat until tender, about 5-7 minutes.
2. **Make sauce**: In a bowl, whisk together peanut butter, soy sauce, honey, garlic, lime juice, and water until smooth.
3. **Combine**: Pour sauce over cabbage noodles and toss to coat.
4. **Serve**: Garnish with chopped peanuts and green onions.

Cauliflower Fried Rice with Shrimp

Ingredients:

- 4 cups cauliflower rice
- 1 lb shrimp, peeled and deveined
- 1 cup mixed vegetables (peas, carrots, corn)
- 2 eggs, beaten
- 3 tbsp soy sauce (or tamari for gluten-free)
- 2 tbsp sesame oil
- 2 green onions, sliced

Instructions:

1. **Cook shrimp**: In a large skillet, heat sesame oil over medium heat. Add shrimp and cook until pink, about 3-4 minutes. Remove and set aside.
2. **Cook vegetables**: In the same skillet, add mixed vegetables and cook until tender. Push to one side and scramble the eggs on the other side.
3. **Combine**: Add cauliflower rice and cooked shrimp back to the skillet. Pour in soy sauce and mix until heated through.
4. **Serve**: Garnish with sliced green onions before serving.

Zucchini Fettuccine with Marinara Sauce

Ingredients:

- 4 medium zucchinis, spiralized into fettuccine
- 2 cups marinara sauce
- 2 tbsp olive oil
- 1/2 tsp Italian seasoning
- Salt and pepper to taste
- Grated Parmesan cheese for serving (optional)

Instructions:

1. **Sauté zoodles**: In a skillet, heat olive oil over medium heat. Add zucchini fettuccine and sauté for 2-3 minutes until just tender.
2. **Add sauce**: Pour marinara sauce over the zoodles and sprinkle with Italian seasoning, salt, and pepper. Cook until heated through.
3. **Serve**: Serve with grated Parmesan cheese if desired.

Feel free to ask if you need more recipes or any further assistance!

Spinach and Feta Stuffed Eggplant

Ingredients:

- 2 medium eggplants, halved
- 2 cups fresh spinach, chopped
- 1 cup feta cheese, crumbled
- 1/2 cup breadcrumbs (gluten-free if desired)
- 1/4 cup onion, diced
- 2 cloves garlic, minced
- 2 tbsp olive oil
- Salt and pepper to taste

Instructions:

1. **Preheat oven**: Preheat the oven to 375°F (190°C).
2. **Prepare eggplant**: Scoop out the insides of the eggplant halves, leaving a 1/2-inch border. Chop the removed flesh and set aside.
3. **Sauté filling**: In a skillet, heat olive oil over medium heat. Add onion and garlic, cooking until soft. Stir in chopped eggplant flesh and spinach until wilted.
4. **Mix filling**: Remove from heat and mix in feta cheese and breadcrumbs. Season with salt and pepper.
5. **Stuff eggplant**: Fill eggplant halves with the mixture and place in a baking dish. Bake for 25-30 minutes until tender.

Spaghetti Squash with Meatballs

Ingredients:

- 1 medium spaghetti squash
- 1 lb ground beef or turkey
- 1/2 cup breadcrumbs (gluten-free if desired)
- 1 egg
- 1/4 cup Parmesan cheese, grated
- 2 cups marinara sauce
- Salt and pepper to taste
- Fresh basil for garnish (optional)

Instructions:

1. **Preheat oven**: Preheat the oven to 400°F (200°C).
2. **Prepare squash**: Cut spaghetti squash in half, scoop out seeds, and place cut side down on a baking sheet. Roast for 30-40 minutes until tender.
3. **Make meatballs**: In a bowl, mix ground meat, breadcrumbs, egg, Parmesan, salt, and pepper. Form into meatballs and place on a baking sheet.
4. **Cook meatballs**: Bake meatballs for 20-25 minutes until cooked through.
5. **Combine**: Scrape out spaghetti squash strands, mix with marinara sauce, and top with meatballs. Garnish with basil if desired.

Egg Noodles with Alfredo Sauce

Ingredients:

- 8 oz egg noodles
- 1 cup heavy cream
- 1/2 cup Parmesan cheese, grated
- 2 tbsp butter
- 2 cloves garlic, minced
- Salt and pepper to taste
- Fresh parsley for garnish (optional)

Instructions:

1. **Cook noodles**: Boil egg noodles according to package instructions. Drain and set aside.
2. **Make sauce**: In a skillet, melt butter over medium heat. Add garlic and sauté for 1 minute. Pour in heavy cream and bring to a simmer.
3. **Add cheese**: Stir in Parmesan cheese until melted and smooth. Season with salt and pepper.
4. **Combine**: Toss cooked noodles with Alfredo sauce until coated.
5. **Serve**: Garnish with fresh parsley if desired.

Cheesy Broccoli and Cauliflower Bake

Ingredients:

- 2 cups broccoli florets
- 2 cups cauliflower florets
- 1 cup cheddar cheese, shredded
- 1/2 cup cream cheese
- 1/2 cup milk
- 1/4 cup breadcrumbs (optional)
- Salt and pepper to taste

Instructions:

1. **Preheat oven**: Preheat the oven to 350°F (175°C).
2. **Blanch vegetables**: In a pot of boiling water, blanch broccoli and cauliflower for 3-4 minutes. Drain and place in a baking dish.
3. **Make sauce**: In a saucepan, melt cream cheese and milk together until smooth. Stir in cheddar cheese until melted. Season with salt and pepper.
4. **Combine**: Pour cheese sauce over vegetables and mix. Top with breadcrumbs if desired.
5. **Bake**: Bake for 25-30 minutes until bubbly and golden.

Zoodle Taco Salad

Ingredients:

- 4 medium zucchinis, spiralized
- 1 lb ground beef or turkey
- 1 packet taco seasoning
- 1 cup cherry tomatoes, halved
- 1 cup black beans, drained and rinsed
- 1/2 cup corn
- 1 avocado, diced
- Salsa and sour cream for serving

Instructions:

1. **Cook meat**: In a skillet, cook ground meat over medium heat until browned. Stir in taco seasoning and water as per packet instructions.
2. **Prepare zoodles**: In a separate skillet, sauté zoodles for 2-3 minutes until just tender.
3. **Assemble salad**: In a bowl, layer zoodles, cooked meat, cherry tomatoes, black beans, corn, and avocado.
4. **Serve**: Top with salsa and sour cream as desired.

Radish Pasta with Lemon Garlic Sauce

Ingredients:

- 4 cups radishes, spiralized
- 2 tbsp olive oil
- 2 cloves garlic, minced
- 1/4 cup lemon juice
- Salt and pepper to taste
- Fresh parsley for garnish

Instructions:

1. **Sauté radishes**: In a skillet, heat olive oil over medium heat. Add spiralized radishes and sauté for 4-5 minutes until tender.
2. **Make sauce**: Stir in garlic and cook for 1 minute. Add lemon juice, salt, and pepper.
3. **Combine**: Toss radish pasta with the lemon garlic sauce.
4. **Serve**: Garnish with fresh parsley before serving.

Spinach and Mushroom Stuffed Peppers

Ingredients:

- 4 bell peppers, halved and seeded
- 2 cups spinach, chopped
- 1 cup mushrooms, diced
- 1 cup cooked rice (or quinoa)
- 1/2 cup mozzarella cheese, shredded
- 1/4 cup onion, diced
- 2 tbsp olive oil
- Salt and pepper to taste

Instructions:

1. **Preheat oven**: Preheat the oven to 375°F (190°C).
2. **Sauté filling**: In a skillet, heat olive oil over medium heat. Add onion and mushrooms, cooking until soft. Stir in spinach until wilted.
3. **Combine**: In a bowl, mix sautéed vegetables with cooked rice and half the mozzarella. Season with salt and pepper.
4. **Stuff peppers**: Fill halved bell peppers with the mixture and place in a baking dish. Top with remaining mozzarella.
5. **Bake**: Bake for 25-30 minutes until peppers are tender.

Feel free to ask if you need more recipes or any further assistance!

Zucchini and Bacon Frittata

Ingredients:

- 4 large eggs
- 1 cup zucchini, diced
- 4 strips bacon, cooked and crumbled
- 1/2 cup onion, diced
- 1/2 cup bell pepper, diced
- 1/2 cup shredded cheese (cheddar or mozzarella)
- Salt and pepper to taste
- 1 tbsp olive oil

Instructions:

1. **Preheat oven**: Preheat the oven to 375°F (190°C).
2. **Sauté vegetables**: In an oven-safe skillet, heat olive oil over medium heat. Add onion and bell pepper, sautéing until soft. Stir in zucchini and cook for another 2-3 minutes.
3. **Mix eggs**: In a bowl, whisk together the eggs, salt, and pepper. Pour the mixture over the sautéed vegetables.
4. **Add bacon**: Sprinkle crumbled bacon and cheese over the top.
5. **Bake**: Transfer the skillet to the oven and bake for 15-20 minutes, or until the frittata is set.

Eggplant Rollatini

Ingredients:

- 2 medium eggplants, sliced lengthwise into thin strips
- 2 cups ricotta cheese
- 1 cup mozzarella cheese, shredded
- 1/2 cup Parmesan cheese, grated
- 1 egg
- 2 cups marinara sauce
- 1 tsp Italian seasoning
- Salt and pepper to taste
- Olive oil for brushing

Instructions:

1. **Preheat oven**: Preheat the oven to 375°F (190°C).
2. **Prepare eggplant**: Brush eggplant slices with olive oil and grill or roast until soft.
3. **Mix filling**: In a bowl, combine ricotta, mozzarella, Parmesan, egg, Italian seasoning, salt, and pepper.
4. **Roll eggplant**: Spread a layer of marinara sauce in a baking dish. Place a spoonful of cheese mixture on each eggplant slice, roll it up, and place seam-side down in the dish.
5. **Bake**: Cover with remaining marinara sauce and bake for 25-30 minutes until bubbly and golden.

Pesto Shirataki Noodles

Ingredients:

- 1 package (8 oz) Shirataki noodles, rinsed and drained
- 1/2 cup pesto sauce (store-bought or homemade)
- 1/4 cup cherry tomatoes, halved
- 1/4 cup Parmesan cheese, grated
- Salt and pepper to taste
- Fresh basil for garnish (optional)

Instructions:

1. **Prepare noodles**: In a skillet, heat Shirataki noodles over medium heat for 2-3 minutes to remove excess moisture.
2. **Add pesto**: Stir in pesto sauce, cooking for another 2 minutes until heated through.
3. **Combine**: Add cherry tomatoes and toss to combine. Season with salt and pepper.
4. **Serve**: Transfer to a plate, top with Parmesan cheese, and garnish with fresh basil if desired.

Feel free to reach out if you need more recipes or any additional assistance!

www.ingramcontent.com/pod-product-compliance
Lightning Source LLC
LaVergne TN
LVHW081341060526
838201LV00055B/2783